# SHORT WALKS LAKE DISTRICT
## CONISTON & LANGDALE

by Paddy Dillon

*View from the summit of the Old Man (Walk 8)*

# CONTENTS

**Using this guide** .................................................................. 4
**Route summary table** ............................................................ 6
**Map key** ........................................................................... 7
**Introduction** ...................................................................... 9
  Walking in the Lake District ................................................... 9
  Where to stay ................................................................... 10
  Travel .......................................................................... 11

**The walks**

| | | |
|---|---|---|
| 1. | Coniston circuit .................................................... | 13 |
| 2. | Coppermines Valley ................................................ | 17 |
| 3. | Coniston and Torver ................................................ | 23 |
| 4. | Sunny Bank to Coniston ............................................ | 29 |
| 5. | Hawkshead to Coniston ............................................ | 35 |
| 6. | Coniston and Tarn Hows ........................................... | 41 |
| 7. | Yewdale Fells ....................................................... | 47 |
| 8. | Old Man of Coniston ............................................... | 53 |
| 9. | Tilberthwaite ....................................................... | 59 |
| 10. | Elterwater and Little Langdale .................................... | 65 |
| 11. | Elterwater and Great Langdale ................................... | 71 |
| 12. | Great Langdale ..................................................... | 75 |
| 13. | Mickleden and Oxendale .......................................... | 81 |
| 14. | Stickle Tarn ......................................................... | 87 |
| 15. | Blea Tarn ........................................................... | 91 |

**Useful information** .............................................................. 95

# USING THIS GUIDE

### Routes in this book

In this book you will find a selection of easy or moderate walks suitable for almost everyone, including casual walkers and families with children, or for when you only have a short time to fill. The routes have been carefully chosen to allow you to explore the area and its attractions. There may be some uphill sections, but any sections of challenging terrain can be avoided (except on Walk 8 and a short section on Walk 14). Do bear in mind that conditions can sometimes be wet or muddy underfoot. A route summary table is included to help you choose the right walk.

### Clothing and footwear

You won't need any special equipment to enjoy these walks. The weather in Britain can be changeable, so choose clothing suitable for the season and wear or carry a waterproof jacket. For footwear, comfortable walking boots or trainers with a good grip are best. A small rucksack for drinks, snacks and spare clothing is useful. See www.adventuresmart.uk.

### Walk descriptions

At the beginning of each walk you'll find all the information you need:

- start/finish location, with postcode and a what3words address to help you find it
- parking and transport information, estimated walking time, total distance and climb
- details of public toilets available along the route and where you can get refreshments
- a summary of the key highlights of the walk and what you might see

Timings given are the time to complete the walk at a reasonable walking pace. Allow extra time for extended stops or if walking with children.

The route is described in clear, easy-to-follow directions, with each waypoint marked on an accompanying map extract. It's a good idea to read the whole of the route instructions before setting out, so that you know what to expect.

### Maps, GPX files and what3words

Extracts from the OS 1:25,000 map accompany each route. GPX files for all the walks in this book are available to download at www.cicerone.co.uk/1197/gpx.

What3words is a free smartphone app which identifies every 3m square of the globe with a unique three-word address, e.g. ///destiny.cafe.sonic. For more information see https://what3words.com/products/what3words-app.

## USING THIS GUIDE

### Walking with children

Even young children can be surprisingly strong walkers, but every family is different and you may need to adapt the timings given in this book to take that into account. Make sure you go at the pace of the slowest member and choose a walk with an exciting objective in mind, such as a cave, river, waterfall or picnic spot. Many of the walks can be shortened to suit – suggestions are included at the end of the route description.

### Dogs

Sheep or cattle may be found grazing on a number of these walks. Keep dogs under control at all times so that they don't scare or disturb livestock or wildlife. Cattle, particularly cows with calves, may very occasionally pose a risk to walkers with dogs. If you ever feel threatened by cattle, you should let go of your dog's lead and let it run free.

### Enjoying the countryside responsibly

Enjoy the countryside and treat it with respect to protect our natural environments. Stick to footpaths and take your litter home with you. When driving, slow down on rural roads and park considerately, or better still use public transport. For more details check out www.gov.uk/countryside-code.

## The Countryside Code

### Respect everyone
- be considerate to those living in, working in and enjoying the countryside
- leave gates and property as you find them
- do not block access to gateways or driveways when parking
- be nice, say hello, share the space
- follow local signs and keep to marked paths unless wider access is available

### Protect the environment
- take your litter home – leave no trace of your visit
- do not light fires and only have BBQs where signs say you can
- always keep dogs under control and in sight
- dog poo – bag it and bin it – any public waste bin will do
- care for nature – do not cause damage or disturbance

### Enjoy the outdoors
- check your route and local conditions
- plan your adventure – know what to expect and what you can do
- enjoy your visit, have fun, make a memory

SHORT WALKS LAKE DISTRICT – CONISTON & LANGDALE

# ROUTE SUMMARY TABLE

| WALK NAME | START POINT | TIME | DISTANCE |
|---|---|---|---|
| 1. Coniston circuit | Coniston tourist information centre | 3hr | 7km (4½ miles) |
| 2. Coppermines Valley | Coniston tourist information centre | 3¼hr | 7.5km (4¾ miles) |
| 3. Coniston and Torver | Coniston tourist information centre | 4hr | 10.5km (6½ miles) |
| 4. Sunny Bank to Coniston | Torver Common above Sunny Bank | 2hr | 6.5km (4 miles) |
| 5. Hawkshead to Coniston | Hawkshead Grammar School | 3hr | 7km (4½ miles) |
| 6. Coniston and Tarn Hows | Coniston tourist information centre | 4hr | 10.5km (6½ miles) |
| 7. Yewdale Fells | Coniston tourist information centre | 4hr | 9.5km (6 miles) |
| 8. Old Man of Coniston | Coniston tourist information centre | 4½hr | 8.5km (5¼ miles) |
| 9. Tilberthwaite | Tilberthwaite | 3hr | 7km (4½ miles) |
| 10. Elterwater and Little Langdale | Elterwater | 3hr | 7km (4½ miles) |
| 11. Elterwater and Great Langdale | Elterwater | 2½hr | 6km (3¾ miles) |
| 12. Great Langdale | New Dungeon Ghyll Hotel, Great Langdale | 3hr | 7km (4½ miles) |
| 13. Mickleden and Oxendale | Old Dungeon Ghyll Hotel, Great Langdale | 3hr | 8km (5 miles) |
| 14. Stickle Tarn | New Dungeon Ghyll Hotel, Great Langdale | 2¼hr | 4.5km (2¾ miles) |
| 15. Blea Tarn | Old Dungeon Ghyll Hotel, Great Langdale | 2hr | 5km (3 miles) |

**ROUTE SUMMARY TABLE**

| HIGHLIGHTS |
|---|
| History and heritage close to Coniston |
| Copper mining history and heritage |
| Former slate quarries and an old railway line |
| Cumbria Way, lake views and lake cruises |
| Historic village, museum, farms and woodland |
| Cumbria Way, scenic tarn and walled garden |
| Fine views, old mines, quarries and woodland |
| High fell with slate quarrying heritage and fine views |
| Herdwick sheep farming and woodland |
| Cathedral Cave and splendid waterfall |
| Classic views, Elterwater and Chapel Stile |
| Cumbria Way, historic hotels, fine fell views |
| Cumbria Way, rugged daleheads and Herdwick sheep |
| Lovely tarn high on the Langdale Pikes |
| Lovely tarn surrounded by high fells |

## SYMBOLS USED ON ROUTE MAPS

 Start point

 Finish point

 Start and finish at the same place

 Waypoint

 Route line

**MAPPING IS SHOWN AT A SCALE OF 1:25,000**

```
0 KM      0.25       0.5
|----|----|----|----|
0 miles        0.25
```

**DOWNLOAD THE GPX FILES FOR FREE AT**
www.cicerone.co.uk/1197/GPX

*The Langdale Pikes (Walk 12)*

# INTRODUCTION

*A direction stone on Elterwater Common (Walk 10)*

In 1835 William Wordsworth said that the Lake District should be 'a sort of national property' for everyone 'who has an eye to perceive and a heart to enjoy'. The National Park was established in 1951, and in 2017 it was further designated as a UNESCO World Heritage Site, as a Cultural Landscape formed by 'the combined works of nature and man'.

Ancient volcanic rocks, 450 million years old, form the high fells of the Lake District, though the shape of the dales is the result of glaciation that ended as recently as 10,000 years ago. Glaciers carved huge hollows high in the Coniston and Langdale fells, which are now filled by tarns. Larger glaciers cut deep into the land, forming the U-shaped Great Langdale. One glacier cut even deeper, scouring out a trough now filled by Coniston Water. Fellsides, woodlands, forests and farmland form an intricate mosaic.

## Walking in the Lake District

Walking in the Lake District is rewarding all year round as the colours of the landscape change dramatically, from Spring when the first flowers emerge and black Herdwick lambs are born, to Autumn when the woodlands and bracken turn russet and gold. Winter, too, brings breathtaking beauty, but care is needed on icy ground. If it rains heavily, find a walk that includes waterfalls!

This guidebook has walks for all seasons and all abilities. Walks 1 to 8 are based around Coniston village. Walk 9 is halfway between Coniston and Great Langdale, and Walks 10 to 15 are based throughout Great Langdale. Most walks are circular, but two are linear, requiring the use of a bus or ferry.

The tracks and paths in this book are usually clear and well signposted, and easy to follow, but occasionally involve steep and rugged slopes. The ascent of the Old Man (Walk 8) is more challenging, and while there is a well-trodden path, the climb to the summit is consistently steep and stony.

## Where to stay

There is plenty of accommodation to suit all pockets. There are campsites at Coniston and Great Langdale and youth hostels at Coniston, Hawkshead and Elterwater. Hotels and B&Bs are plentiful and there are abundant self-catering lets.

### Coniston

Coniston is a bustling village served by daily buses. Coniston Water can be explored on cruises operated all year round by the Coniston Launch, or seasonally by the National Trust Steam Yacht Gondola. There is plenty of accommodation as well as a tourist information centre, museum, pubs, restaurants, cafes, two small supermarkets, and outdoor and gift shops.

### Hawkshead

Hawkshead is a charming old village featuring a maze of narrow streets and poky alleyways, fun to explore and full of interesting places offering food and drink. The poet William Wordsworth was educated at Hawkshead Grammar School, which is now a museum.

### Little Langdale

This quiet dale contains few facilities apart from a pub, occasional teas in a scenic garden, and maybe an opportunity to select a home-made cake from a farmyard stall.

### Elterwater

This little village is the gateway to Great Langdale, served by daily buses. There is accommodation, a pub, cafe and nearby hotels with restaurants.

### Great Langdale

Chapel Stile has a pub, shop and cafe, while the New and Old Dungeon Ghyll Hotels both offer accommodation, food and drink. There are two campsites – one at Baysbrown Farm near Chapel Stile and the other closer to the Old Dungeon Ghyll Hotel.

*Coppermines Youth Hostel, a former mine manager's house*

## Travel

### Rail
Use West Coast mainline trains to reach Lancaster or Oxenholme, then local services. Although there are regular trains from Lancaster to Ulverston, there are only two opportunities, weekdays only, to catch the X112 bus onwards from Ulverston to Coniston. Trains from Oxenholme reach Kendal or Windermere, connecting with regular daily bus services.

### Bus
Bus stops are located beside the railway terminus at Windermere. Some buses run directly to Coniston (Stagecoach 505) or Langdale (Stagecoach 516), but most operate from Ambleside, in which case catch any bus from Windermere to Ambleside, including Stagecoach 555 for Keswick and 599 for Grasmere. Change buses in Ambleside for Stagecoach 505 to Hawkshead and Coniston, or Stagecoach 516 for Skelwith Bridge, Elterwater, Chapel Stile, New Dungeon Ghyll Hotel and Old Dungeon Ghyll Hotel. With the exception of Walk 9, all walks in this guide can be accessed by public transport.

### Boat
The ferry landings at Coniston and Sunny Bank (for Walk 4) are served by Coniston Launches. The National Trust Steam Yacht Gondola doesn't serve Sunny Bank, but by all means use it for an elegant cruise on the lake.

*Coniston Launch jetty and Bluebird Cafe*

# WALK 1
## Coniston circuit

**Time** 3hr
**Distance** 7km (4½ miles)
**Climb** 150m

**An easy circular walk close to Coniston exploring heritage, waterfalls and the lake**

| | |
|---|---|
| **Start/finish** | *Coniston tourist information centre* |
| **Locate** | *LA21 8EH ///loosens.splinters.buns* |
| **Cafes/pubs** | *Pubs and cafes in Coniston, cafe by the lake, pub at Bowmanstead* |
| **Transport** | *Daily buses from Ambleside to Coniston and weekday buses from Ulverston to Coniston* |
| **Parking** | *Pay and display at Coniston tourist information centre* |
| **Toilets** | *Tourist information centre and Coniston Boating Centre* |

An interesting circuit from Coniston, with fell views, mining heritage, the shore of Coniston Water and part of an old railway track. The only steep climbing comes at the start and everything else is easy. At many points it's possible to cut the walk short and return to the village, where the Ruskin Museum is well worth a visit.

*Coniston seen from near Haws Bank, with the rugged Yewdale Fells beyond*

## SHORT WALKS LAKE DISTRICT – CONISTON & LANGDALE

**1** Start across the road from the tourist information centre and car park, and walk towards the centre of **Coniston**. Cross a bridge over a river and turn right to follow a road up to the Sun Hotel. This 16th-century inn has served packhorse traders and railway travellers throughout the centuries. Turn right after the hotel as signposted for the Old Man and Levers Water. The road becomes a track, crossing a bridge before climbing past Coniston Stonecraft. Follow the track uphill beside woodland, spotting a waterfall in Church Beck before reaching **Miners Bridge**.

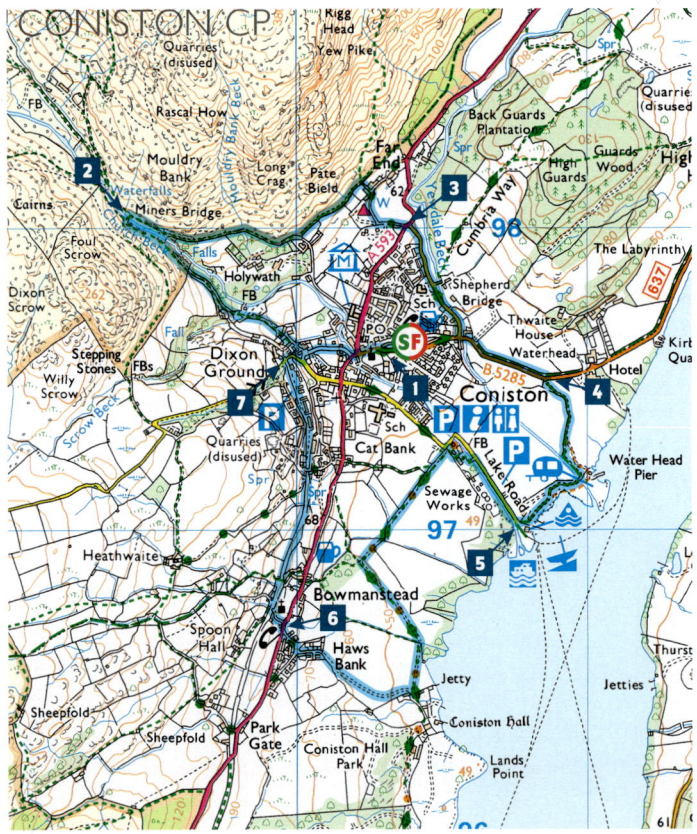

*Waterfall on Church Beck seen after Miners Bridge*

## WALK I – CONISTON CIRCUIT

Yewdale Bridge. Follow a footpath and cycleway parallel to the road. Turn right when signposted across the road for the Coniston Boating Centre.

**4** Follow an access road at first then switch to a path on the right, which later crosses a footbridge. Walk through woodland along the shore of **Coniston Water** to reach the Coniston Boating Centre. The Bluebird Cafe and toilets are here, as well as the Coniston Launch and the Steam Yacht Gondola.

**5** Follow a path between **Lake Road** and a river, crossing a footbridge to reach retail units. Walk between the units to reach a corner on Lake Road, turning left to go through double kissing gates. A signpost indicates a path to Torver, which runs alongside a field, passing through gates, later reaching **Coniston Hall** with its thick stone walls and chunky chimneys. Turn right to walk up the access road from the hall to **Haws Bank**, then keep right to reach the A593 road.

**2** Cross the bridge, go through a gate and turn right down a rough-surfaced road. Cross a cattle grid and turn left through a gate signposted for Yew Tree Farm. A path descends gently beside a drystone wall. Turn right through a gate, dropping between buildings to a road at **Far End**, and turn right again. Follow the road past Holly How youth hostel to a crossroads.

**3** Go straight through the crossroads along Shepherds Bridge Lane. There are two bridges on the left, Shepherd Bridge and one for Coniston Sports and Social Club, but don't cross either. Instead walk to the end of the lane and turn left along the **B5285 road** signposted for Tarn Hows, crossing

**6** Cross over the road and follow a narrow road up past the Church of the Sacred Heart, passing beneath a bridge. Turn right, go through a gate, and immediately turn left along the track of an old railway. There is access down to the Ship Inn nearby at Bowmanstead, if required. The track

*16th-century Coniston Hall*

passes beneath a stone arch and leads to houses, workshops and the Old Station car park.

**7** Turn right down a road, then left for the Sun Hotel, and right to continue back into **Coniston**. Cross a bridge and pass St Andrew's Church to finish back at the tourist information centre.

> **— To shorten**
> Make your way directly back to Coniston from almost any point on the circuit.

### The Ruskin Museum

One of the great visionaries of the Victorian era, John Ruskin was – among other things – an artist, art critic, writer, social critic and philosopher. The Ruskin Museum in Coniston was founded in 1901 by Ruskin's secretary, W G Collingwood. There are spaces dedicated to geology and archaeology, arts and crafts, John Ruskin and the author Arthur Ransome. The museum was extended to include an exhibition devoted to Donald Campbell (who in the 1950s and 60s broke the World Water Speed Record several times on Coniston Water ) and his speedboat 'Bluebird' (ruskinmuseum.com).

# WALK 2
## Coppermines Valley

| | |
|---|---|
| **Start/finish** | Coniston tourist information centre |
| **Locate** | LA21 8EH ///loosens.splinters.buns |
| **Cafes/pubs** | Pubs and cafes in Coniston |
| **Transport** | Daily buses from Ambleside to Coniston and weekday buses from Ulverston to Coniston |
| **Parking** | Pay and display at Coniston tourist information centre |
| **Toilets** | Tourist information centre |

**Time** 3¼hr
**Distance** 7.5km (4¾ miles)
**Climb** 380m

**Mining and quarrying heritage on the steep and rugged slopes of the Coppermines Valley**

This walk climbs from Coniston to the dramatic and scenic Coppermines Valley. Despite being pitted and scarred, with heaps of colourful rock waste, the heritage is remarkable. German and Irish miners toiled there, and informative notices enable visitors to interpret the ruins. Paths pick their way across steep slopes and occasional chunky blocks of slate are carved with historical notes.

*Industrial heritage at the Coniston Coppermines*

*Paths pick their way across steep slopes in the shadow of the fells*

**1** Start across the road from the tourist information centre and car park, and walk towards the centre of **Coniston**. Pass between the Black Bull Inn and Co-op Village Store, continuing past the Ruskin Museum. Follow the road uphill, cross a cattle grid, climb beside Church Beck with its waterfall and pass **Miners Bridge**. Reach a stout slate block carved with 'Land of Power and Ore'.

**2** Turn right at a junction beside the stone, following a track uphill. Turn right again to avoid a terrace of houses known as Irish Row. Climb past slate spoil then, when the track bends sharp right, turn left instead up a lesser track. Another stout slate block is passed at the site of the Bonsor East Wheel House. The next wheel house features a stone tower. Cross a wooden bridge over a beck in the **Red Dell** and turn left.

*Old quarry track climbing above Irish Row in the Coppermines Valley*

*The enormous Pudding Stone*

(i) *A Herdwick sheep's year involves lambing (April), shearing (July), dipping (September) and tipping (November), when male 'tips' are introduced to female 'yows'.*

**Before turning left you can walk ahead a short way to read a notice about the 'Wheel of Misfortune', where an accident resulted in the death of Thomas Millican in 1850.**

**3** Turn left away from the bridge and watch carefully to find and follow a narrow path running beside an old ditch. This man-made 'leat' was cut to carry water to waterwheels. Follow the leat across the fellside, level most of the time, except for a short stretch avoiding a small tunnel. Follow a path left and right across a rugged slope to skip the tunnel and follow the leat to join a stony track. Turn right and walk up the track to reach a dam at **Levers Water**.

**4** Use a few steps to cross a granite lip on the dam, though this isn't possible after heavy rain. If the lip can't be crossed, cut the walk short by going back down the track, past the Coppermines youth hostel, to return to Coniston. After crossing the dam, pass a fenced-off mineshaft and turn left to walk straight up a short, steep slope, crossing a gap at 440m. Follow a path down into **Boulder Valley**, crossing a footbridge to pass the huge **Pudding Stone**.

## WALK 2 – COPPERMINES VALLEY

**5** The path rises a little before going down a rocky slope. Reach an old slate quarry and follow its access track past juniper bushes on **Crowberry Haws**. Reach a junction with a popular path climbing the Old Man (Walk 8) and turn left downhill, then shortly afterwards turn left down another path.

**6** The path descends through a gate in a fence, crosses the fellside and goes through a gate in a drystone wall, closely followed by another gate in another drystone wall. Keep following the path, enjoying views of the Coppermines Valley. Go through a gate and pass **Miners Bridge**. Don't cross the bridge, but follow a track straight ahead, going through a gate and passing below Coniston Stonecraft. The track drops and crosses a bridge, passing houses to reach the Sun Hotel. Turn left and follow the road down to **Coniston**.

### – To shorten
The stony track from Levers Water runs straight down to Coniston if needed, saving about 15min.

## Copper mining

Copper was mined in this valley in fits and starts from the 16th to the 20th century. German miners were brought into the area in the 16th century, but production was disrupted during the English Civil War. During the 18th century, waterpower allowed mines to be sunk deeper. Peak production came in the 19th century,

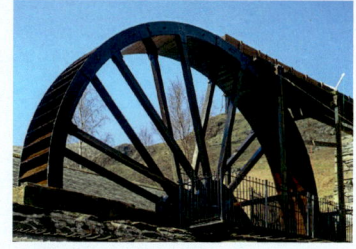

*Restored waterwheel at the Coniston Coppermines*

followed by a swift decline and the end of the industry in the early 20th century. A splendid restored waterwheel, often seen turning, can be inspected at the Coniston Coppermines, along with other industrial artefacts.

*Trackbed of the old Coniston railway passing beneath a stone arch*

# WALK 3
## Coniston and Torver

| | |
|---|---|
| **Start/finish** | *Coniston tourist information centre* |
| **Locate** | *LA21 8EH ///loosens.splinters.buns* |
| **Cafes/pubs** | *Pubs and cafes in Coniston, pub and take-away at Torver (350m off route), pub at Bowmanstead* |
| **Transport** | *Daily buses from Ambleside to Coniston and weekday buses from Ulverston to Coniston* |
| **Parking** | *Pay and display at Coniston tourist information centre or Old Station* |
| **Toilets** | *Tourist information centre* |

After a steep climb from Coniston, the Walna Scar Road rises gently across the lower slopes of the Old Man. A grassy path links with quarry and farm tracks to Torver. The return walk follows an old railway track back to Coniston, but you could catch a bus back, as long as you time your arrival correctly at Torver.

**Time** 4hr
**Distance** 10.5km (6½ miles)
**Climb** 315m

**Follow quarry tracks to Torver and a railway track back to Coniston**

*The Walna Scar Road runs all the way from Coniston to the Duddon Valley*

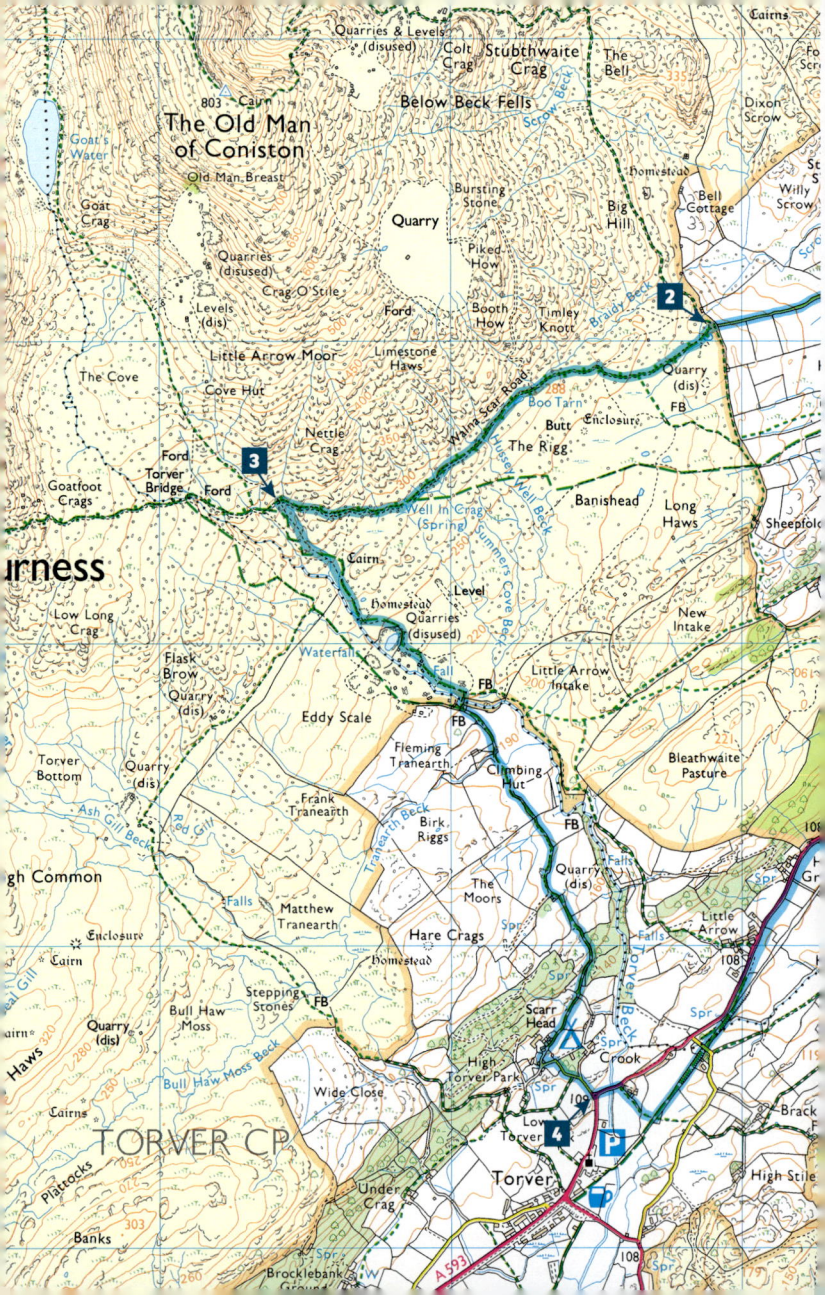

## WALK 3 – CONISTON AND TORVER

**1** Start across the road from the tourist information centre and car park, and walk towards the centre of **Coniston**. Cross a bridge over a river and turn right to follow a road up to the Sun Hotel. Turn right at a road junction above the hotel then climb steeply up a wooded slope. The road later climbs gently past fields, reaching a gate and car park.

**2** Walk straight ahead along the gravel **Walna Scar Road**. The track rises gently then later climbs steeply through a rock cutting. Further uphill follow the track through another rock cutting and reach two wooden posts, one either side of the track, at around 340m. Turning right leads to Goat's Water, for a longer walk.

**3** Turn left down a grassy path on a bracken slope. Pass the fenced-off edge of Bannisdale Quarry, where a waterfall can be seen. Follow the path down past slate spoil to where a slate sign points you right, across a bridge. Continue through gates and two sheepfolds to follow an obvious track gently downhill. Cross a concrete bridge below a house and the track undulates with

25

*The grassy path descending from the Walna Scar Road*

good views of the fells. Walk down past a barn and follow the track to houses at **Scarr Head**. A minor road leads down to the A593 road. **Torver** is 5min to the right, but to continue the walk, turn left. X112 buses stop for a clear signal.

**4** Follow the main road across a bridge to a nearby house and turn right through a kissing gate. Keep to the left-hand side of a field, go through a gap in a fence and walk a short way up to a signpost. Turn left along the track of an old railway.

**The railway linked Coniston, Torver and Broughton-in-Furness to the coastal railway at Foxfield. Created to transport slate and copper away from Coniston from 1859, it brought tourists to and from the area before closing in 1962.**

> ⓘ *Norse-derived placenames include beck (stream), dale (valley), fell (mountain), force (waterfall), gill (ravine), lang (long), tarn (lake), thwaite (clearing).*

## WALK 3 – CONISTON AND TORVER

Pass beneath a stone arch and follow the track until diverted onto the main road at **Little Arrow**. Follow a roadside path until a right turn leads into a wood to rejoin the old railway line. Follow it through woods and along part of the access road for **Park Coppice** caravan site. The old track continues until it reaches a blocked-off bridge and is forced back onto the A593 road.

**5** Walk a short way down the road, turn left, then immediately right through a gate to pick up and follow the old track once more. It passes the Church of the Sacred Heart at **Haws Bank**, and there is access to the Ship Inn a short distance away at **Bowmanstead**, if required. Pass under an arched bridge to reach the Old Station car park and workshop units. Turn right at a road junction, pass the Sun Inn and return to the centre of **Coniston** to finish.

### − To shorten
Catch the weekday X112 bus from Torver back to Coniston, saving about 4km (1hr 30min).

### + To lengthen
Turn right instead of left at Waypoint 3 to follow a path up to Goat's Water, just under 3km (1hr) there and back, with 160m extra ascent.

*Slate quarry spoil passed on the way to Torver*

Coniston Water from the shoreline path near Sunny Bank

# WALK 4
## Sunny Bank to Coniston

**Time** 2–2½hr
**Distance** 6.5 or 5.5km (4 or 3½ miles)
**Climb** 100m

**Follow the Cumbria Way along the scenic western shore of Coniston Water**

| | |
|---|---|
| **Start** | Torver Common above Sunny Bank, or Sunny Bank jetty |
| **Finish** | Coniston tourist information centre or Coniston Boating Centre |
| **Locate** | LA21 8BL ///patching.alright.petal or ///crouching.camps.commander |
| **Cafes/pubs** | Pubs and cafes in Coniston, cafe at boating centre |
| **Transport** | Weekday buses from Coniston or Ulverston to Sunny Bank. Summer launch to Sunny Bank jetty |
| **Parking** | Pay and display at tourist information centre or boating centre |
| **Toilets** | Coniston tourist information centre and Coniston Boating Centre |

Sunny Bank can be reached either by bus, or by taking the Coniston Launch along the lake. The walk goes along the wooded shoreline of Coniston Water, so views are especially good in the winter when there is no foliage. The shoreline path is obvious and easy, but the route drifts away from the lake on the final approach to Coniston.

*Coniston Hall seen from the campsite*

# SHORT WALKS LAKE DISTRICT – CONISTON & LANGDALE

**1** If using the Coniston Launch, boats leave the Coniston Boating Centre. If catching a bus, ask the driver for the lay-by above **Sunny Bank**. A signpost reads 'Coniston via Lake Shore'. Follow a track over a gentle rise and go through a kissing gate, then follow a path down to **Coniston Water**. The

*Looking along Coniston Water from near Hoathwaite*

Coniston Launch serves a wooden jetty at this point for those coming by boat.

**2** There's only one shoreline path, which is obvious, though narrow and stony in places, rising and falling, passing wooded and open areas on **Torver Back Common**. Enjoy lake views and pass birch, oak, holly and gorse bushes until you reach a little gate in a fence. Watch for a mound of dark slag just before crossing Moor Gill, the site of a medieval iron-smelting 'bloomery'.

**3** Enter a well-wooded area. Later, go through a little gate in a drystone wall, entering tall forest where many trees have been blown over, and look for another 'bloomery' site. The path is enclosed by fences and criss-crossed by tree roots as it passes **Torver**

*Fragments of slag from medieval iron-smelting*

**Common Wood**, reaching a wooden jetty served by the Coniston Launch.

**4** Cross a footbridge and go through a large gate in a drystone wall. Follow a path through woodland. Cross another footbridge and go through a gate in a drystone wall, passing a boathouse and jetty at **Hoathwaite Landing**. Follow a track past boats, then go through a gate in a fence and keep right of a grassy area to go through a gate in a fence. Continue along the shore path past a signpost for Coniston, followed by a footbridge and double gates through a drystone wall.

**5** Go through the gates and follow the path through a large pasture, with fine views of the Old Man, Swirl How, Wetherlam and Fairfield. Go through a gate in a drystone wall, then follow a tarmac road through a campsite that's busy in summer and empty in winter. Pass **Coniston Hall** and its stout chimneys.

**6** Turn right, leaving the tarmac road to follow a clear track through fields. This gives way to a path with a firm surface, passing through gates and later going through double kissing gates to reach a corner on **Lake Road**,

> ⓘ *Peel Island, towards the southern end of Coniston Water, was the inspiration for Wild Cat Island in the* Swallows and Amazons *books.*

# WALK 4 – SUNNY BANK TO CONISTON

close to retail units. Turn right to visit the units or to return to the Coniston Boating Centre, otherwise turn left for Coniston.

**7** Lake Road has a pavement and passes the John Ruskin School to reach a crossroads. Turn right to walk into **Coniston**, crossing a bridge to reach the centre near St Andrew's Church. Keep right to return to the tourist information centre.

### – To shorten

An early finish is possible by catching the Coniston Launch from the Torver jetty, giving a walk of just over 2km (45min). Alternatively, start at the Torver jetty and walk back to the Boating Centre, a distance of just under 3.5km (1hr 15min).

### + To lengthen

Leaving Coniston Hall, switch to Walk 1 for a slightly longer route to Coniston via an old railway track (adds 5min).

## Swallows and Amazons

Arthur Ransome combined Coniston Water and Windermere to form an ideal lake for the *Swallows and Amazons* children's adventure stories. The crew of the 'Swallow' are John, Susan, Titty and Roger Walker. The crew of the 'Amazon' are Nancy and Peggy Blackett. The stories have been adapted for both film and television. For lake cruises either sail on the Gondola (www.nationaltrust.org.uk/visit/lake-district/steam-yacht-gondola) or the Coniston Launch (www.conistonlaunch.co.uk).

*The 'Amazon' (formerly 'Mavis') partially inspired Arthur Ransome*

*Tall conifers on the approach to the head of Coniston Water*

# WALK 5
## Hawkshead to Coniston

| | |
|---|---|
| **Start** | *Opposite Hawkshead Grammar School* |
| **Finish** | *Coniston tourist information centre* |
| **Locate** | *LA22 0NT ///trifling.fingertip.menu* |
| **Cafes/pubs** | *Pubs and cafes in Hawkshead and Coniston* |
| **Transport** | *Daily buses from Ambleside link Hawkshead and Coniston* |
| **Parking** | *Pay and display at Hawkshead, or park at Coniston tourist information centre and take bus to Hawkshead* |
| **Toilets** | *At Hawkshead and beside Coniston tourist information centre* |

**Time** 3hr
**Distance** 7km (4½ miles)
**Climb** 200m

**A lovely, easy walk from Hawkshead to Coniston through fields and forests**

This is a linear walk linking ancient Hawkshead, with its maze of poky alleyways, to Coniston. Both villages have museums and repay careful exploration. There are opportunities to catch buses in either direction at four intermediate bus stops if the walk needs to be cut short for any reason.

*Slate slabs between fields around Hawkshead*

## SHORT WALKS LAKE DISTRICT

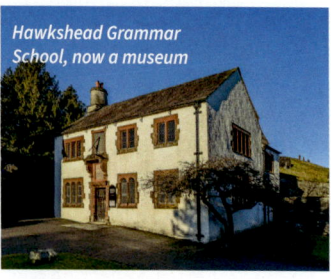

*Hawkshead Grammar School, now a museum*

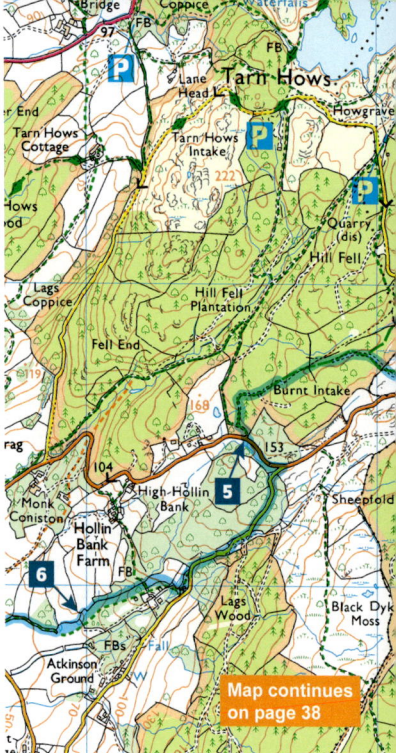

Map continues on page 38

**1** Start at the bus stop in **Hawkshead**, which bears a signpost for 'Vicarage Lane via Church'. Cross the road and go up past Hawkshead Grammar School to reach St Michael and All Angels Church. Go through a churchyard gate, then slate slabs flank a path between fields. Go through another gate, turn right through another field, go through yet another gate and pass Dolly's Community Orchard. Vicarage Lane leads to a road junction at **Walker Ground**.

**2** Turn left as signposted for Coniston, then turn right at stone gateposts. Walk across a field and turn left uphill beside a fence, signposted for Tarn Hows. Climb past fields and forest, go through gates, follow a stream and cross a concrete slab. Walk up a stony path and climb steps through a gate. Walk up through a field and cross a farm access road. Climb further, then go down to a kissing gate and turn left along the B5285 road to **Hawkshead Hill**.

**3** Pass Hawkshead Hill Baptist Chapel. Turn right at a road junction and bus stop, as signposted for Tarn Hows. Keep left at two road junctions then almost immediately turn right, signposted for Tarn Hows. Watch on the left for a kissing gate and signpost for Tarn Hows and follow a path rising parallel to the road. It veers away from the road on bushy slopes. Two kissing gates are reached at the corner of a drystone wall.

*Wharton Tarn, also known as High Cross Tarn*

37

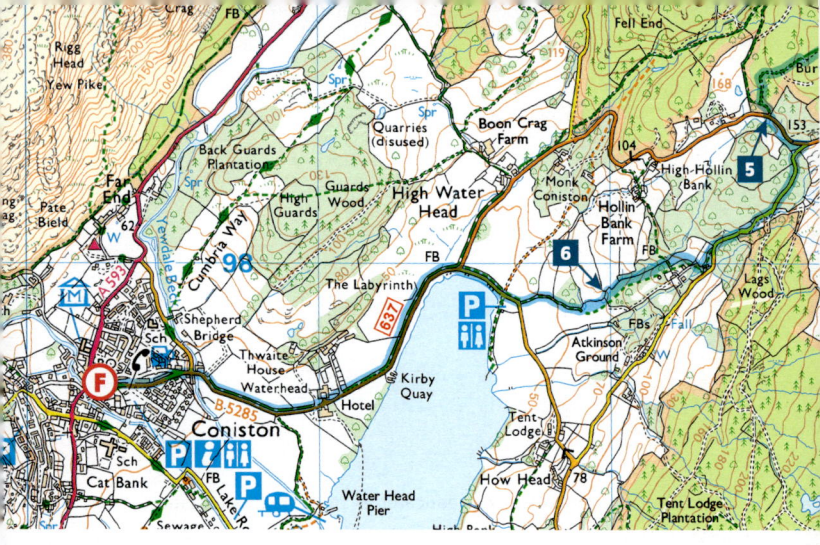

**4** Go through the kissing gate on the left and keep left to follow a dry-stone wall overlooking **Wharton Tarn**. Don't go onto the road at **High Cross**, but note that buses will stop here if needed. Keep right as signposted for Coniston down a winding path. Go through a gate in a drystone wall near the tarn and walk up into a wood. A path gives way to a forest track at **Burnt Intake**. The track descends and a left turn leads to the B5285 road and a bus stop at Holling Brow.

**5** Turn left up the road, facing oncoming traffic, then turn sharp right along a road signposted 'East of Lake'. Follow the road down through woods and keep right down an access road for Rowlandson Ground. Cross a stream and turn right up 23 slate steps. Walk through woods and descend 32 wooden steps, and finally go down 46 concrete steps.

**6** Emerge from the woods and walk down through a field. Turn right through a kissing gate, cross slate slabs over a stream and follow a stony path. This can be like a streambed after rain but soon leads to a road. Turn right to walk along a path parallel to the road, passing the Monk Coniston car park. A nearby jetty is used by the Gondola and Coniston Launch. Cross a road junction at the head of **Coniston Water**. The path running parallel to the road is used by walkers and cyclists, and apart from a break at The Coniston Inn, where there are bus stops, it leads all the way to **Coniston**. Follow the road straight into the village.

**WALK 5 – HAWKSHEAD TO CONISTON**

### – To shorten
Catch a bus at one of the bus stops mentioned in the route description at Hawkshead Hill, High Cross, Holling Brow and The Coniston Inn.

### + To lengthen
Turn right at the kissing gate before Wharton Tarn to walk to a viewpoint for Tarn Hows, 1.5km (30min) there and back.

## Hawkshead

The pretty village of Hawkshead contains old buildings and poky alleyways to explore, as well as offers of food and drink. The 18th-century poet William Wordsworth was educated at Hawkshead Grammar School, which now serves as a museum illustrating school life from 1585 to 1909 (www.hawksheadgrammar.org.uk).

*Jetty at Monk Coniston car park*

*Yewdale Beck near Low Yewdale, looking towards the Yewdale Fells*

# WALK 6
## Coniston and Tarn Hows

**Time** 4hr
**Distance** 10.5km (6½ miles)
**Climb** 330m

**Exploring Tarn Hows and the Monk Coniston estate**

| | |
|---|---|
| **Start/finish** | Coniston tourist information centre |
| **Locate** | LA21 8EH ///loosens.splinters.buns |
| **Cafes/pubs** | Pubs and cafes in Coniston |
| **Transport** | Daily buses from Ambleside to Coniston and weekday buses from Ulverston to Coniston |
| **Parking** | Pay and display at Coniston tourist information centre or Sports and Social Centre |
| **Toilets** | Coniston tourist information centre and car park at Tarn Hows |

The Cumbria Way long-distance footpath runs from Coniston to Tarn Hows, passing Tarn Hows Cottage, which once belonged to Beatrix Potter. A circuit of the popular and scenic tarn is included, but could be omitted for a shorter walk. For a quiet walk, visit in the winter. The return to Coniston runs through forest and passes a splendid arboretum and walled garden at Monk Coniston.

*Tarn Hows Cottage with the Tilberthwaite valley beyond*

# SHORT WALKS LAKE DISTRICT – CONISTON & LANGDALE

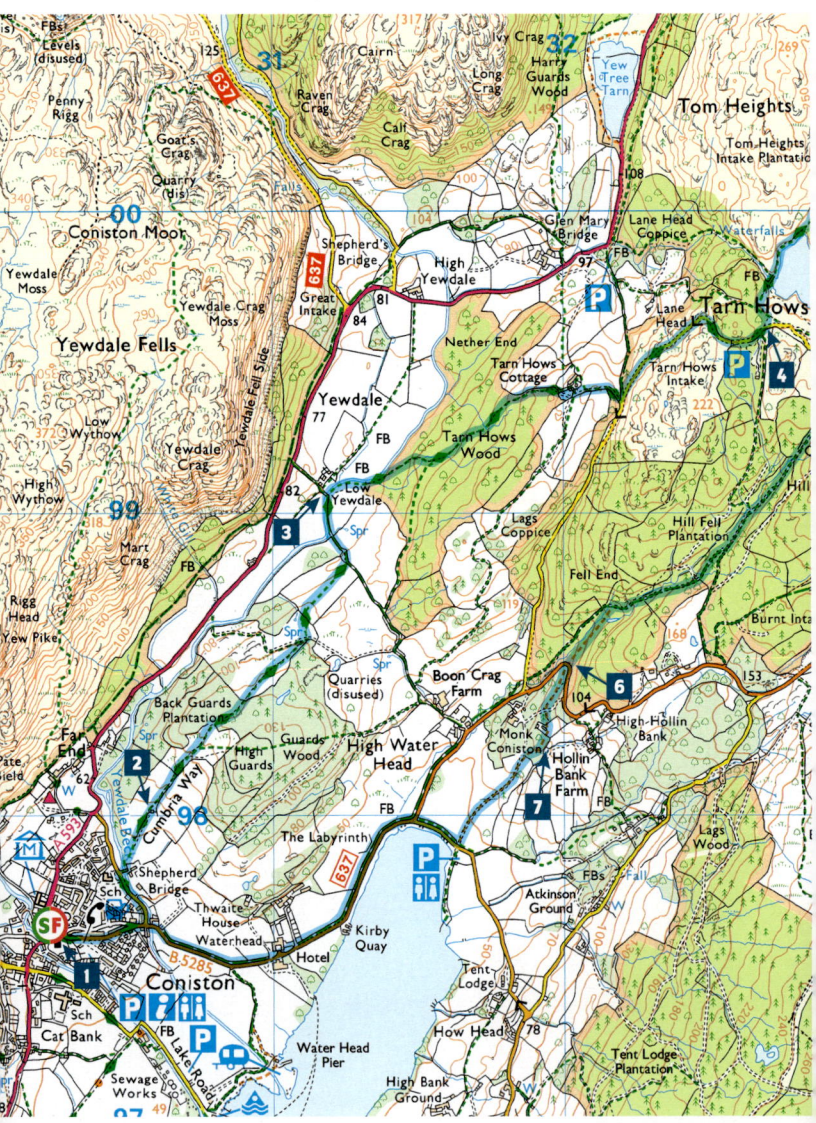

## WALK 6 – CONISTON AND TARN HOWS

**1** Start across the road from the tourist information centre and car park. Walk out of **Coniston** towards Hawkshead. Turn left along Shepherds Bridge Lane and pass Coniston Sports and Social Centre. Turn right to cross **Shepherd Bridge** and immediately turn left along a path. Climb through a field to reach the Dog House. What looks like a miniature castle turns out to be an ornate former kennel, now a shelter.

*The castle-like Dog House is a former kennel*

## SHORT WALKS LAKE DISTRICT – CONISTON & LANGDALE

**2** Walk up from the Dog House and go through a gate. Keep left when the path splits, walking uphill through a kissing gate into a wooded area. Follow a path downhill and keep left through another kissing gate. Keep straight ahead and go through a gate. Turn left to follow a track to a bridge at **Low Yewdale**.

**3** Don't cross the bridge, but turn right through a kissing gate. Walk across a field and go through another kissing gate, then climb through **Tarn Hows Wood**. Cross a footbridge and continue uphill. Go through a gate to reach **Tarn Hows Cottage**. Follow the access road and turn left up a road to reach the National Trust car park.

**4** Turn left, away from the car park, following a path down to a gate on a small dam at **Tarn Hows**. The path makes a complete circuit around the tarn, passing wooded and open areas. After crossing a footbridge at the head of the tarn, the path runs through **Rose Castle Plantation**, then splits. Turn left up a broad path signposted for Hawkshead, going through a gate and later reaching a car park and a road.

**5** Cross the road, go through a big gate and walk down a forest path. Turn left at a junction, as signposted for Coniston. Keep straight ahead at the next junction for Coniston. After a level stretch, turn right for Coniston, then keep straight ahead at other junctions downhill, crossing a stream. Turn left, signposted for Monk Coniston, down a few steps to cross a small dam. Follow a path down to the **B5285** road and cross with care.

**6** Go through a gate and follow a woodland path towards **Monk Coniston**. Turn left at a huge sequoia

*Tarn Hows is encircled by an easy path*

## Tarn Hows

*Tarn Hows in winter with a view of Wetherlam beyond*

Three small pools were known as The Tarns until the 1860s, when the owner of the Monk Coniston estate, James Marshall, dammed them to create one large tarn. The impounded water powered a sawmill. The area was purchased by Beatrix Potter before it passed to the National Trust. This is an incredibly popular visitor attraction, although its beauty was somewhat marred in recent years after a number of diseased larches had to be felled.

tree and go through a gate into a walled garden. You can visit the Potting Shed for information, or go through another gate to leave the garden. A short detour to the right leads to the Gazebo, which offers information about the Monk Coniston estate.

**7** If not visiting the Gazebo, walk straight down from the garden, through a gate and straight down a field to a road. Turn right to walk along a path, crossing a road junction at the head of **Coniston Water**. The path running parallel to the road is used by walkers and cyclists, and apart from a break at The Coniston Inn, where there are bus stops, it leads all the way to **Coniston**. Follow the road into the village.

### — To shorten

Stay on the road to omit the path encircling Tarn Hows and rejoin the route at Waypoint 5, saving almost 3km (1hr).

*Row of cottages at Tilberthwaite*

# WALK 7
## Yewdale Fells

| | |
|---|---|
| **Start/finish** | Coniston tourist information centre |
| **Locate** | LA21 8EH ///loosens.splinters.buns |
| **Cafes/pubs** | Pubs and cafes in Coniston |
| **Transport** | Daily buses from Ambleside to Coniston and weekday buses from Ulverston to Coniston |
| **Parking** | Pay and display at Coniston tourist information centre, or free parking beside the Church Beck road |
| **Toilets** | Coniston tourist information centre |

**Time** 4hr
**Distance** 9.5km (6 miles)
**Climb** 450m

**A longer walk over the Yewdale Fells to Tilberthwaite with a return through woodland**

After climbing alongside Church Beck into the Coppermines Valley, a path formerly used by miners and quarrymen leads past the Yewdale Fells to a deep ravine and former slate quarries in Tilberthwaite. Keep children close to you near steep rocky slopes and quarry edges at Tilberthwaite. An easy low-level route leads back to Coniston.

*Looking towards the Fairfield Horseshoe from the path to Tilberthwaite*

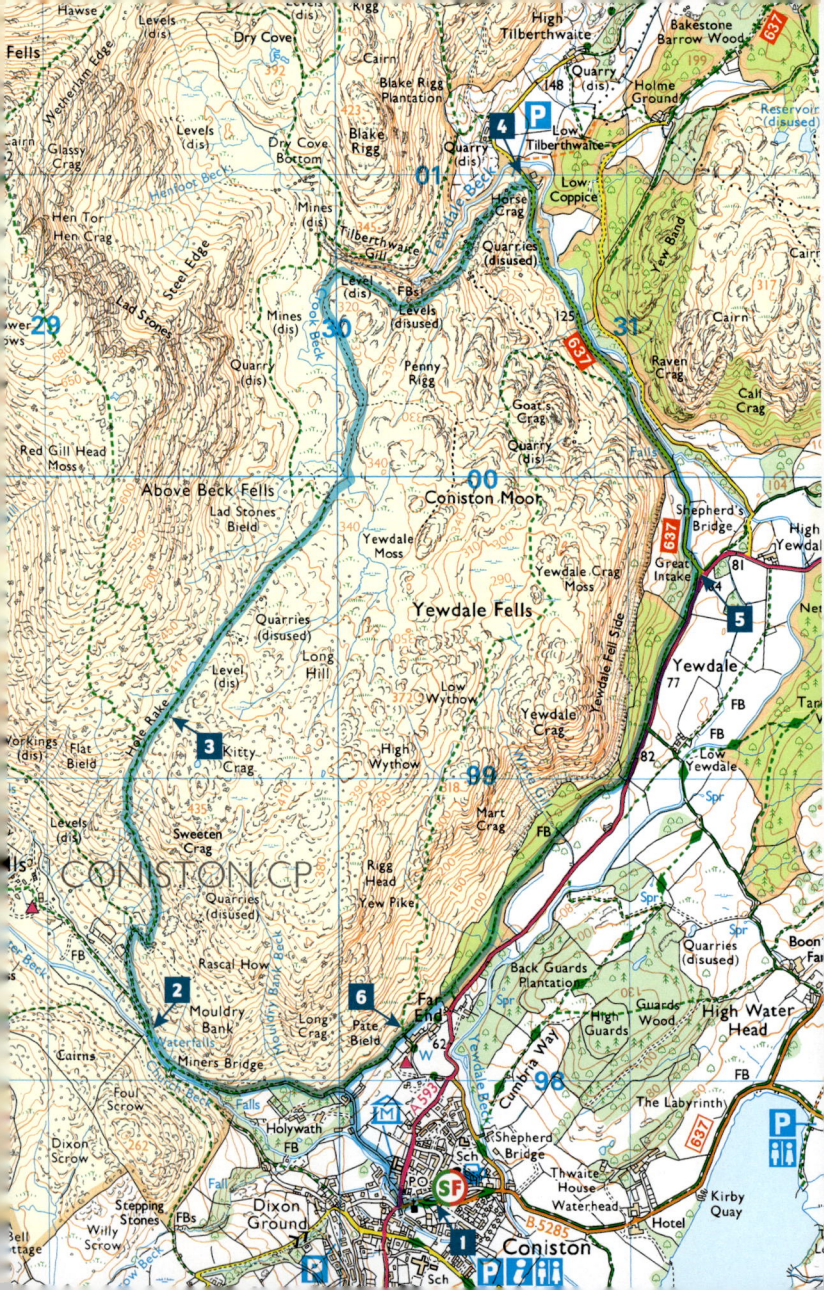

*Hole Rake beside the rugged Yewdale Fells*

**1** Start across the road from the tourist information centre and its car park, and walk towards the centre of **Coniston**. Pass between the Black Bull Inn and Co-op Village Store, continuing past the Ruskin Museum. Follow the road uphill, cross a cattle grid, climb beside Church Beck, admiring a waterfall as you go, and pass **Miners Bridge**. Reach a stout slate block carved with 'Land of Power and Ore'.

**2** Turn right at a junction beside the stone, following a track uphill. Turn right again to avoid a terrace of houses. Climb past slate spoil and when the track bends sharp right follow it a little further, then turn left up a narrow, stony path flanked by bracken. There are short flights of stone steps and the path eventually climbs into a high valley at **Hole Rake**, around 410m, passing between the **Yewdale Fells** and distant Wetherlam.

**3** Keep straight ahead along the most obvious path, passing small quarries or mines. Views ahead include Helvellyn, with Fairfield and High Street later. The path descends gently

*A path rises gently through woods to return walkers to Coniston*

> ⓘ *Lake District slates might look grey, but they are often described as 'green' or 'blue', and some of them reveal striking patterns when cut and polished.*

and crosses a stream, then becomes a bit muddy as it swings right near the ravine of **Tilberthwaite Gill**. Stay on the path, passing a cairn on a mine spoil heap. Take care on a short rocky scramble then the path passes close to an unfenced quarry edge. Pass slate spoil and go down 35 slate steps to reach a car park at **Low Tilberthwaite**.

**4** Across the road is a sheepfold sculpture by the artist Andy Goldsworthy. However, to continue the walk follow the road to the right. It is bendy, and rises and falls, so keep an eye out for traffic while enjoying the rugged fells and woodland. Reach a junction with the A593 road at **Great Intake**.

**5** Turn right, not along the main road but along an obvious path running parallel, often screened from the road by trees at the foot of **Yewdale Fell Side**. The path is open to walkers and cyclists and it later climbs away from the road and crosses three footbridges. Emerge from the woods to walk alongside a drystone wall, passing above houses and Holly How youth hostel at **Far End**.

**6** The path and drystone wall lead to a gate giving access to a steep, rough-surfaced road. This was used earlier in the day, so turn left to walk down it, and it soon gains a tarmac surface, levelling out to pass the Ruskin Museum on its way back into **Coniston**.

> ⓘ *Herdwick sheep have a strong 'hefting' instinct, which means that they seldom wander from the fellsides they grazed as lambs with their mothers.*

## Andy Goldsworthy sheepfolds

Andy Goldsworthy is an English sculptor, photographer and environmentalist. The sheepfold on this walk is called the Tilberthwaite Touchstone Fold. The circular slate structures built into the four walls are angled to reflect light in different ways. Other examples of Andy Goldsworthy's sheepfold art can be discovered all around Cumbria – see www.sheepfoldscumbria.co.uk for more details.

*Looking down on Low Water from the stone-paved path*

# WALK 8
## Old Man of Coniston

**Time** 4½hr
**Distance** 8.5km (5¼ miles)
**Climb** 750m

**Climb the highest of the Coniston Fells for fine views, and study the quarrying heritage**

| | |
|---|---|
| **Start/finish** | Coniston tourist information centre |
| **Locate** | LA21 8EH ///loosens.splinters.buns |
| **Cafes/pubs** | Pubs and cafes in Coniston |
| **Transport** | Daily buses from Ambleside to Coniston and weekday buses from Ulverston to Coniston |
| **Parking** | Pay and display at Coniston tourist information centre, or Walna Scar Road car park for shorter walk |
| **Toilets** | Coniston tourist information centre |

The Old Man of Coniston, Coniston Old Man, or just the Old Man, features a steep but obvious path. Quarrymen once trudged up and down the path in all weathers and evidence of their toil is plain to see. Generations of tourists have followed in their steps in the hope of extensive views from the summit. If the climb isn't going well for any reason, simply turn around and walk back down.

*The steep and rocky lower slopes of the Old Man*

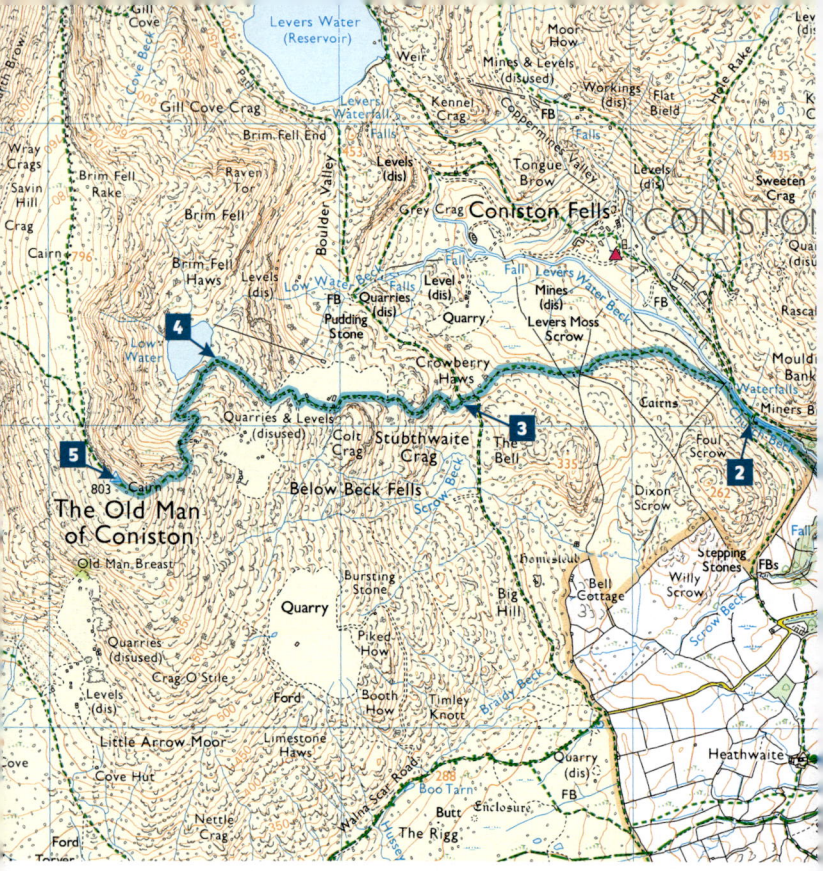

**1** Start across the road from the tourist information centre and car park, and walk towards the centre of **Coniston**. Cross a bridge over a river and turn right to follow a road up to the Sun Hotel. Turn right after the hotel, as signposted for the Old Man and Levers Water. The road becomes a track, crossing a bridge before climbing past Coniston Stonecraft. Follow the track uphill beside woodland, spotting a waterfall in **Church Beck** before reaching **Miners Bridge**.

> ⓘ *The 'Wainwrights' are 214 Lake District fells described by Alfred Wainwright in a series of guidebooks first published between 1955 and 1966.*

## WALK 8 – OLD MAN OF CONISTON

walk from the Walna Scar Road car park joins here. Turn right and follow the track a short way uphill to reach a junction of paths at **Crowberry Haws**, at 310m.

**3** Keep left at the junction to climb a steep, stone-paved or boulder-strewn path. It winds uphill, passing rocky outcrops and the spoil heaps of old **quarries**. Pass rusty cables, reaching a level area around 450m where the ruins of old sheds, winding gear and railway lines can be inspected at Saddlestone Quarry. Keep climbing, passing more rusty cables and quarries. Turn right

**2** Don't cross the bridge, but continue upstream, emerging from the wood to go through a gate in a drystone wall. There is a fine view of the Coppermines Valley from here. The path climbs across a slope of bracken and later passes through another two gates in drystone walls. Climb further and follow the path through a gate in a fence, joining a clear track. A shorter

*Rail tracks and old winding gear at Saddlestone Quarry*

55

*A dusting of snow on the Old Man and a distant view towards the Yorkshire Dales and Lancashire*

at a junction, rather than approaching a toppled pylon. Climb further for a sudden view of **Low Water**, at almost 550m. This makes a splendid picnic site.

**4** The path keeps climbing, zigzagging up chunky stone steps on the higher slopes of the fell, where quarrying is evident to 650m. The path becomes steep and rocky, though some parts feature slabs and steps. Stick to the obvious path to reach a huge cairn on top of the **Old Man of Coniston**, with a trig point alongside at 803m.

> Views from the top of the Old Man embrace the Coniston Fells, the rest of the Lake District, Yorkshire, Lancashire, and possibly North Wales, the Isle of Man and Southern Scotland.

**5** The safest way to finish is to retrace your steps all the way down to **Coniston**. Take care on steep, rocky parts and it should take less time to go down than it did to climb.

## The Old Man

Most visitors hear some tale explaining where the 'Old Man' got its name. An oft-repeated story says it derives from a Celtic root – *Allt Maen* – meaning 'high cliff'. However, even the foremost local placename authority W G Collingwood concluded that most opinions were pure guesswork.

### – To shorten

Start from the Walna Scar Road pay and display car park (see Walk 3), and take the path signposted for Coniston Old Man, saving a total of 2km (45min) and 180m of ascent.

*Light snowfall between Holme Ground and High Tilberthwaite*

# WALK 9
## Tilberthwaite

| | |
|---|---|
| **Start/finish** | Tilberthwaite car park |
| **Locate** | LA21 8DG ///protrude.angry.scooter |
| **Cafes/pubs** | Three Shires Inn (700m off-route) and High Park tea garden (500m off-route) |
| **Transport** | No public transport |
| **Parking** | Honesty car park at Tilberthwaite |
| **Toilets** | No public toilets on route |

A car is required to access Tilberthwaite, where there are no services for visitors. Woodland screens quarries and spoil heaps from view, and there are small farms dotted through the valley, with High Tilberthwaite specialising in Herdwick sheep. A short detour allows Hodge Close Quarry to be entered, which features a spacious cavern and a deep pool of water.

**Time** 3hr
**Distance** 7km (4½ miles)
**Climb** 220m

**Walk around the farms, woodland and slate quarries of Tilberthwaite**

*The farmhouse at Low Tilberthwaite has a well-preserved spinning gallery*

**1** Access for cars is from the A593 road between Coniston and Skelwith Bridge, taking a minor road signposted for Tilberthwaite. A car park with an honesty box lies at the foot of a slate spoil heap before **Low Tilberthwaite**. Start walking along the road past the farm, noticing an old spinning gallery. The tarmac ends at the next farm, **High Tilberthwaite**. Walk through the farmyard and keep right to leave it and follow a clear track onwards.

**2** The track runs uphill and downhill a short way, passing woods and fields, with a distant view of Red Screes. The valley is drained by **Pierce How Beck**, but the track soon runs into woodland and views are limited. Heaps of slate spoil remind visitors that there are quarries nearby. The track eventually passes a house and reaches a signposted junction. Straight ahead is a bridge giving access to Little Langdale and the Three Shires Inn.

**3** Turn sharp right as signposted for Elterwater and Ambleside, staying in the woods. The track becomes a tarmac road crossing a bridge, then climbing steeply to cross a cattle grid to reach farm buildings at **Stang End**. There is an option to follow the road another 500m off-route to High Park tea garden. Turn right uphill, as signposted for Hodge Close and Coniston.

*View of Little Langdale from above Stang End*

Tarmac gives way to a stony track that passes through gates on a slope that is alternately wooded or rugged on **Little Fell**. After a downhill stretch, reach houses at **Hodge Close**.

**4** Turn left up a track signposted 'Public Way High Oxen Fell'. Note that Hodge Close Quarry is on the right.

> The quarry at Hodge Close has precipitous cliffs and a deep, dark pool. A steep and rocky path allows cautious visitors to enter, passing through a cavern on the approach to the pool near the flooded quarry bottom.

> ⓘ *Herdwick lambs are born black. Their fleece turns brown as they grow, finally becoming grey as they mature, providing naturally coloured wool.*

Avoiding the quarry, walk up through a gate on a wooded slope. Turn right through a gate as signposted for Holme Ground and Yewdale. Pass close to the fenced-off quarry, follow the path up through a gate and continue uphill beside a drystone wall. The path levels out, overlooking a terrace of houses.

*The cavern at Hodge Close slate quarry*

*Andy Goldsworthy's 'Touchstone Fold' sculpture at Tilberthwaite*

**5** Go through a gate and follow the drystone wall down across a slope. A track on the right goes down to Holme Ground, but keep straight ahead instead, following a track that rises and goes through a gate on the wooded slopes of **Yew Band**. The track runs down through a gate to join a road.

**6** Turn sharp right to follow the bendy road as it rises through woods at **Low Coppice**. Turn left as signposted along a footpath, through a gate and into the woods. A path leads down to a gate – go through it to continue straight across a field. Go through another gate and walk beside a drystone wall to reach the farm access road just left of **High Tilberthwaite**. Turn left and follow the road back to the car park. Look across the road to spot a sheepfold sculpture (see Walk 7).

> **+ To lengthen**
>
> Add a little extra road-walking to visit the Three Shires Inn or High Park tea garden.

Britannia Inn, Elterwater

# WALK 10
## Elterwater and Little Langdale

| | |
|---|---|
| **Start/finish** | Britannia Inn, Elterwater |
| **Locate** | LA22 9HP ///prank.herb.either |
| **Cafes/pubs** | Pub, cafe and restaurant at Elterwater, snacks at Dale End, tea garden at High Park |
| **Transport** | Daily buses from Ambleside to Elterwater |
| **Parking** | Pay and display at Elterwater, limited free parking on the common |
| **Toilets** | Elterwater |

**Time** 3hr
**Distance** 7km (4½ miles)
**Climb** 260m

**A walk from Elterwater to lovely Little Langdale featuring a slate footbridge, a cavern and a waterfall**

An interesting walk from Great Langdale to Little Langdale, taking in woodland, fine fell scenery and a rustic footbridge that used to be crossed by quarrymen working in Little Langdale. There is an opportunity to visit Cathedral Cave in an old slate quarry, as well as the lovely waterfall of Colwith Force.

*A clear track links Elterwater with Little Langdale*

## SHORT WALKS LAKE DISTRICT – CONISTON & LANGDALE

**1** Start in **Elterwater** near the Britannia Inn. An old farmhouse was converted into an inn in the 19th century to serve local quarrymen and visiting tourists. Walk down the road past the car park to cross a bridge over Great Langdale Beck. Pass Elterwater Hostel and Eltermere Inn and turn right up a road signposted as a cycleway to Coniston. It says 'challenging option',

> ⓘ *The Cumbria Way runs for 113km through the Lake District, from Ulverston, through Coniston and Langdale, and on to Carlisle.*

which is true for cyclists as the road becomes a steep and stony track. Climb through woods, pass through

*Slater Bridge in Little Langdale*

gates and later pass fields, with Wetherlam in view ahead from **Howe Banks**. After a level stretch the track drops to **Dale End**, where take-away snacks are sometimes available.

**2** Walk down the farm road to reach a junction with another road. Turn left then almost immediately right along the Birk Howe Farm road. Just before the farm, turn right through a gate and follow a path beside a drystone wall. Enjoy views over Little Langdale Tarn, and soon reach the slabs and stone arch of **Slater Bridge**. Cross the bridge and then a small field to reach a track.

**3** Turn left and soon reach a junction with another track, with a locked gate and a stile alongside.

There is an option to cross the stile, go up the track and walk through a short tunnel to visit Cathedral Cave in an old quarry.

**A notice warns that the cave is dangerous, but cautious visitors will proceed with care. The cavern beyond is remarkable and is supported by a stout column of slate.**

If not visiting the cave, follow the main track through **Little Langdale**, reaching a bridge and a **ford**. A 700m detour leads across the bridge and along the road to the Three Shires Inn.

**4** Turn right then immediately left as signposted for Elterwater and Ambleside, staying in the woods. The track becomes a tarmac road, crossing a bridge and climbing steeply to cross a cattle grid to reach farm buildings at **Stang End**. Follow the road to the next buildings at **High Park** and keep left to pass between them as signposted. There is a tea garden here, where drinks and cakes are sometimes available, but if you are not stopping go through a gate marked for the Cumbria Way. Follow a field path onwards, reaching a gate into a wood. Immediately on entering the wood, there are paths to left and right. Right is easier, while left is more awkward, but left offers views of **Colwith Force** waterfall. Both paths join a road.

*Cathedral Cave in Little Langdale*

*High Park, where tea and cakes are sometimes available*

**5** Turn left to follow the road over a bridge and keep straight ahead at a junction, signposted for Elterwater, squeezing between buildings at **High Colwith** and **Low Colwith**. Follow the road into woodland until a track and a gate are spotted on the left. A signpost reads 'Elterwater avoiding road'.

**6** Follow the track into the wood and turn right along a path. Simply walk through **Fletcher's Wood**, roughly parallel to the road, avoiding any path or track that climbs left.

Eventually, a concrete track is reached at a water treatment works. Walk down to the road and turn left, passing the Eltermere Inn and Elterwater Hostel to return to **Elterwater**.

### + To lengthen

It's possible to follow the Cumbria Way from Colwith to Skelwith Bridge and from there back to Elterwater, adding an extra 2km (1hr) to the day's walk.

*Looking up Great Langdale Beck towards the Langdale Pikes*

# WALK 11
## Elterwater and Great Langdale

| | |
|---|---|
| **Start/finish** | Britannia Inn, Elterwater |
| **Locate** | LA22 9HP ///prank.herb.either |
| **Cafes/pubs** | Pub, cafe and restaurant at Elterwater, pub and cafe at Chapel Stile |
| **Transport** | Daily buses from Ambleside to Elterwater and Chapel Stile |
| **Parking** | Pay and display at Elterwater, limited free parking on the common |
| **Toilets** | Elterwater and Chapel Stile |

**Time** 2½hr
**Distance** 6km (3¾ miles)
**Climb** 130m

**Easy low-level walking in Great Langdale between Elterwater and Chapel Stile**

A well-wooded farm road leaves Elterwater and as the trees thin out, Great Langdale is gradually revealed, with the distinctive shape of the Langdale Pikes dominating the valley, never likely to be confused with any other fells. Slate quarries are very evident around Elterwater and Chapel Stile.

*Looking back along the level track near Baysbrown Farm*

**SHORT WALKS LAKE DISTRICT – CONISTON & LANGDALE**

**1** Start in **Elterwater** and walk down the road past the car park to cross a bridge over Great Langdale Beck. Pass Elterwater Hostel and Eltermere Inn and turn right up a road signposted as a cycleway to Coniston. The sign says 'challenging option', which is true for cyclists as the road becomes a steep and stony track. However, walkers keep right along a farm access road on gentler gradients in **Sawrey's Wood**. The road rises and falls a little and the woodland screens slate quarries from view. A solitary house is passed in the woods and the road later runs past fields to reach **Baysbrown Farm**.

**2** Keep left to walk through the farmyard, passing a sign for Oak Howe attached to a boulder to reach more wooded slopes. Turn right to leave the track as signposted for Great Langdale and follow a clear path through the woods, then continue through gates from one rugged field to another. The path later swings right and keeps right at a junction to pass a farm at **Oak Howe.**

**3** Follow the farm access road, which runs level through fields and soon runs beside **Great Langdale Beck**. Pass a campsite field near Baysbrown

*Three-way signpost behind farm buildings at Oak Howe*

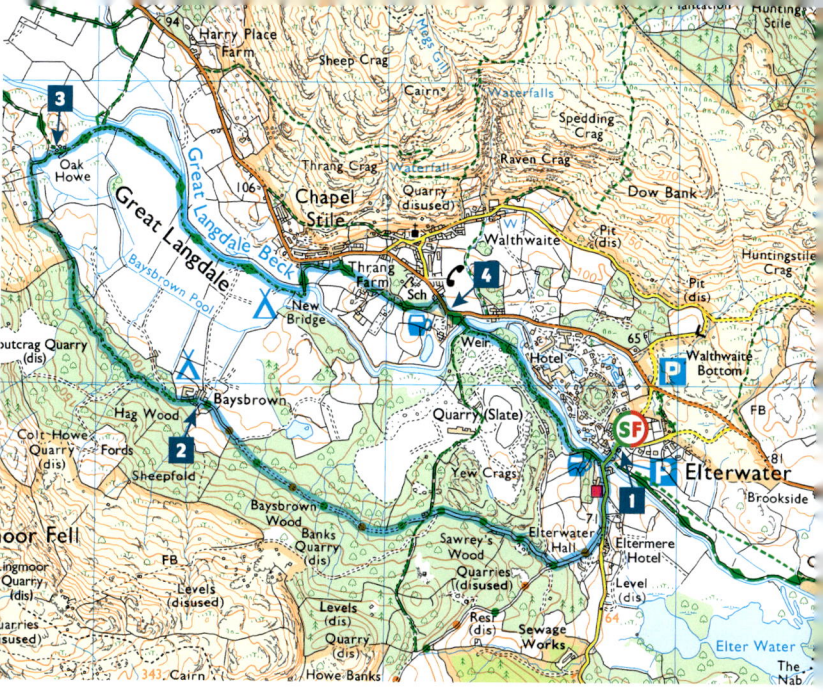

Farm, then make a sudden left turn across **New Bridge**. Follow the road onwards and it bends right, but when it suddenly turns left to join the B5343 road, turn right instead along a track to **Thrang Farm**. This bendy track runs behind the rugged grounds of Langdale Primary School, joining the B5343 road in **Chapel Stile**. There are toilets almost immediately opposite, with the Co-op village store and Brambles Cafe just to the left. Turn right to reach Wainwrights' Inn.

**4** Just after passing the inn, turn right to find a metal footbridge spanning

ⓘ *Lake District slates aren't true slates, in the sense of being metamorphosed mudstone or shale, but are formed of fine-grained volcanic ash.*

**Great Langdale Beck**. Cross over and turn left as if to follow a riverside path. This soon veers away from the river and climbs beside slate spoil to reach a quarry road. Turn left to follow the road and it soon leads to a bridge. Turn left to cross it and return to **Elterwater**.

*The little village of Chapel Stile*

> ### ✚ To lengthen
> From Oak Howe (Waypoint 3), follow Walk 12 further on through Great Langdale, where you can catch a bus at either New or Old Dungeon Ghyll, adding 1hr–1hr 30min to the walk.

## Chapel Stile and Elterwater

Both villages were once tiny, but expanded to house quarrymen and gunpowder workers in the 19th century. Before Holy Trinity Church was built at Chapel Stile, deceased dalesfolk were carried over to Grasmere for burial. Following the closure of the gunpowder works between both villages in 1930, the site was redeveloped as a hotel, timeshare and spa complex.

# WALK 12
**Great Langdale**

| | |
|---|---|
| **Start/finish** | *Bus stop near New Dungeon Ghyll Hotel, Great Langdale* |
| **Locate** | *LA22 9JX ///pods.nurses.boil* |
| **Cafes/pubs** | *Pub restaurants at the New and Old Dungeon Ghyll Hotels and Lanty Slee's* |
| **Transport** | *Daily buses from Ambleside to New and Old Dungeon Ghyll* |
| **Parking** | *Pay and display near New and Old Dungeon Ghyll Hotels* |
| **Toilets** | *Close to Lanty Slee's and at Old Dungeon Ghyll Hotel* |

**Time** 3hr
**Distance** 7km (4½ miles)
**Climb** 170m

**Easy low-level walking with splendid views of the Langdale Pikes**

A level and easy track runs along the floor of Great Langdale. A stretch of the Cumbria Way follows a fellside path linking Oak Howe and Side House. The distinctive profile of the Langdale Pikes remains in view throughout the walk, with other notable fells moving in and out of view.

*Grassy pastures at the head of Great Langdale*

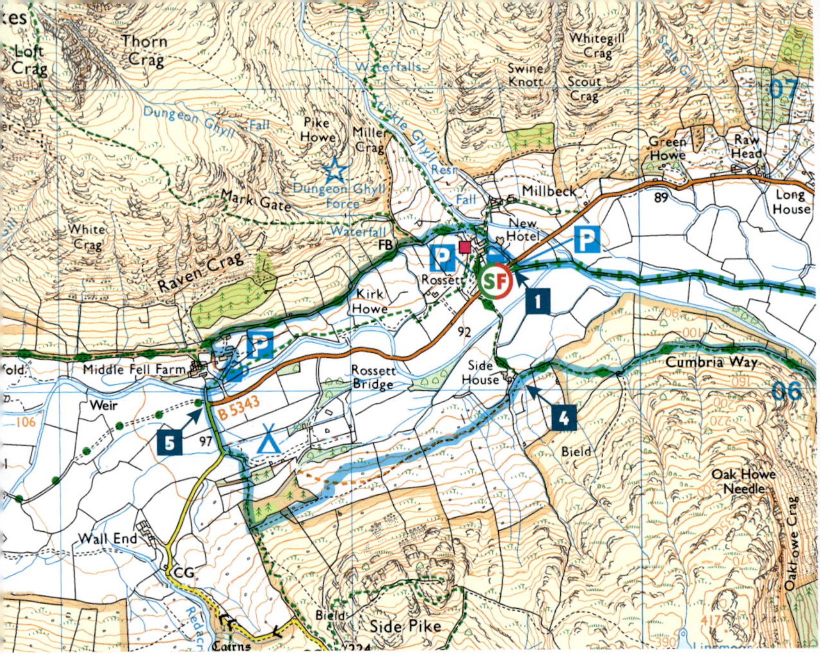

*The New Dungeon Ghyll Hotel*

## WALK 12 – GREAT LANGDALE

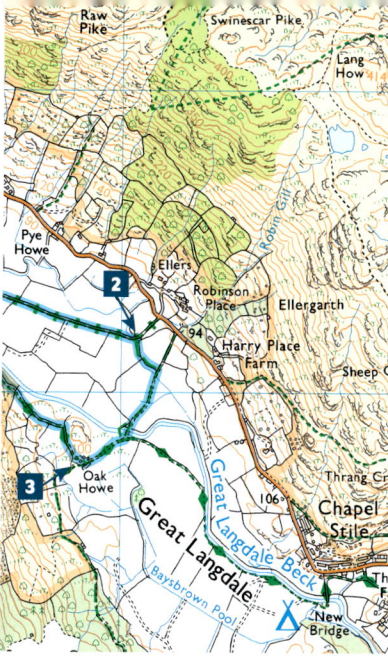

over **Great Langdale Beck**. Turn right to follow a track past the farm of **Oak Howe**, reaching a three-way signpost.

**3** Turn right as signposted for New Dungeon Ghyll. The path later passes through a gate and often has a drystone wall alongside. It's quite rough and stony as it rises on the lower slopes of Lingmoor Fell. Eventually, you reach a gate where there is a fine view of Great Langdale. Go through the gate and walk down a stone-paved path, almost reaching the farm at **Side House**.

**4** Turn left, looking uphill a little to spot a ladder stile over a drystone wall. Follow a faintly trodden path from field to field, crossing other ladder stiles, then pass along the top side of a small forest plantation. When the forest fence reaches a drystone wall, turn right through a kissing gate and walk down through the forest. Go through another kissing gate to continue down a grassy slope, then go through yet another kissing gate to walk down through a wood. Turn left along a track leaving the **Great Langdale Campsite** to reach a road. Turn right and follow the road until it suddenly turns right.

**1** Start at the bus stop or adjacent car park at the **New Dungeon Ghyll Hotel**. Look for a broad and obvious track leaving the car park, signposted as a cycleway to Elterwater and Ambleside. The track briefly follows Great Langdale Beck but mostly passes fields. The track eventually rises towards the B5343 road. Don't follow it quite that far, but look out for a lesser track to the right.

**2** Turn right along the track and walk a short way to join another track. Turn right again, immediately crossing a bridge over a stream, following the track through a field to cross a bridge

**5** Instead of turning right, go straight across a bridge over **Great Langdale Beck**. Turn right along a field path to reach an access road and follow it to the **Old Dungeon Ghyll Hotel**. Walk round the back of the hotel, go up a stony path through a kissing gate then turn right and climb further, following a drystone wall across the lower slopes of the Langdale Pikes. The path is obvious, but sometimes rough and stony, rising and falling, later crossing

*Raven Crag above the Old Dungeon Ghyll Hotel is owned by a climbing club*

*Looking back along the route from above the New Dungeon Ghyll Hotel*

a footbridge. Walk straight ahead and down to the **New Dungeon Ghyll Hotel**.

> ⓘ *The Old Dungeon Ghyll Hotel and New Dungeon Ghyll Hotel are often referred to by the abbreviations ODG and NDG.*

### ▬ To shorten

The walk can be cut short at Side House, using the farm access road to return to the New Dungeon Ghyll Hotel, for a circuit of just over 4km (under 2hr). Or finish at the Old Dungeon Ghyll Hotel and catch a bus.

## Dungeon Ghyll

Dungeon Ghyll is a ravine on the Langdale Pikes containing Dungeon Ghyll Force. The word 'force' derives from the Norse *foss*, meaning 'waterfall'. The word 'gill' derives from the Norse *gil*, meaning 'ravine'. The variant spelling 'ghyll' derives from a poem written by William Wordsworth. He initially used the word 'gill', but a later reprint featured 'ghyll', without any reason being given for the change.

*Looking back down the valley from the head of Mickleden*

**Time** 3hr
**Distance** 8km (5 miles)
**Climb** 130m

**An easy low-level walk in two scenic dales surrounded by high fells**

**Toilets** ... Ghyll Hotel

A stony track runs from the Old Dungeon Ghyll Hotel, passing below the celebrated Langdale Pikes, to reach the head of Mickleden. After you have admired this wild and remote place, the route doubles back and heads for neighbouring Oxendale, which seems even wilder, yet is served by a clear track.

*A good track serves rugged Oxendale*

## SHORT WALKS LAKE DISTRICT – CONISTON & LANGDALE

**1** Start at the bus stop or the car park near the **Old Dungeon Ghyll Hotel**. Walk round the back of the hotel, go up a stony path and through a kissing gate. Follow a very stony path straight ahead. Later, go through another kissing gate beside a big gate. Look back to see Lingmoor Fell, with Blea Tarn pass to the right of it. Pike of Blisco is followed by Crinkle Crags, The Band, Bowfell, Rossett Pike, Pike o' Stickle and Harrison Stickle. Follow the track onwards through **Mickleden** to reach a kissing gate beside a big gate.

**2** Go through the kissing gate and along the broad path. When the drystone wall on the left turns left, there is an option to shorten the walk. Otherwise, keep walking straight onwards, parallel to **Mickleden Beck**,

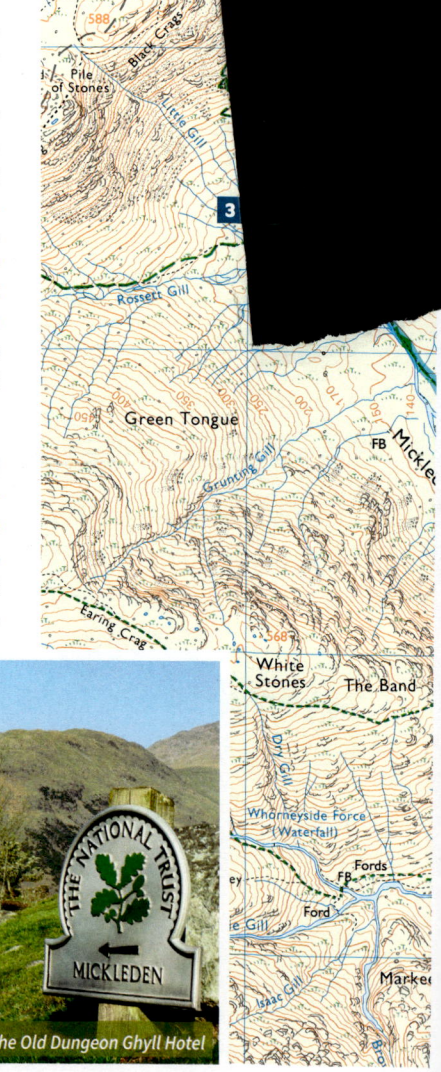

*A stony track leads from the back of the Old Dungeon Ghyll Hotel*

# WALK 13 – MICKLEDEN AND OXENDALE

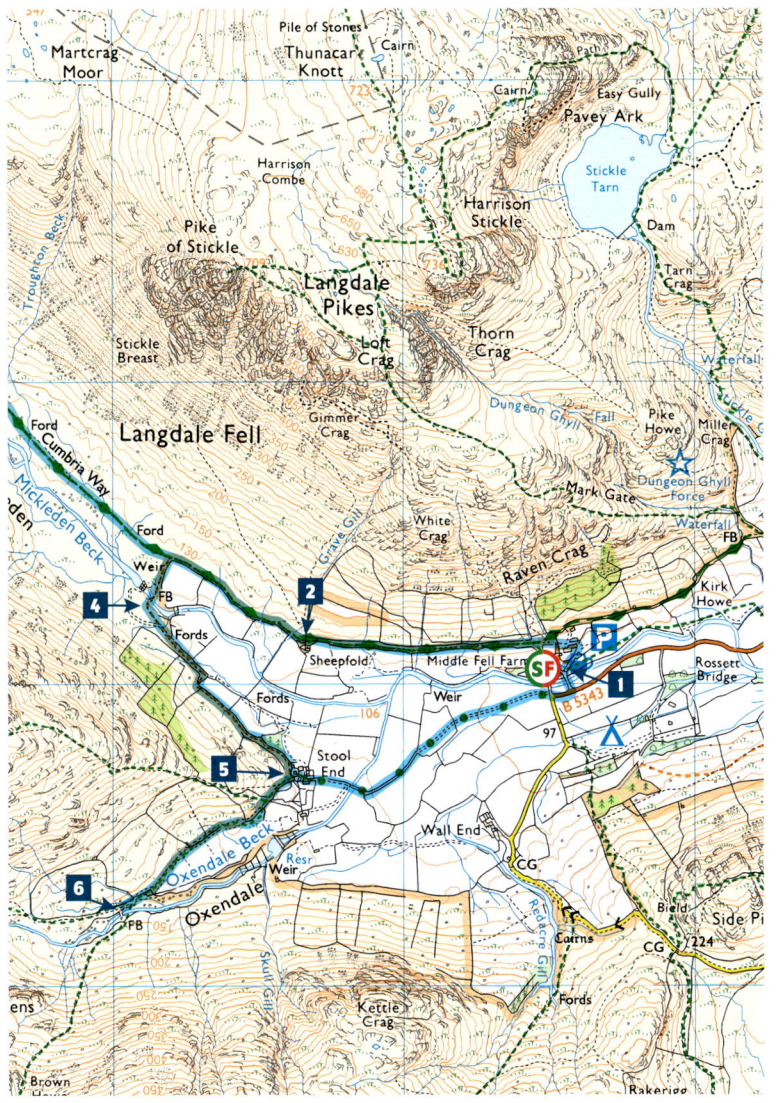

but some distance away from it. Eventually, a footbridge is crossed over **Stake Gill** and a large stone marks the way to Esk Hause and to Stake Pass.

**3** Rather than climb further, turn around to recross the footbridge and retrace your steps through Mickleden. When you reach the corner of the drystone wall passed earlier in the walk, turn right to follow it, then head straight for a footbridge spanning **Mickleden Beck** and cross it.

**4** Climb a little from the footbridge and turn left to follow a path a short way until it reaches a clearer track. Keep straight ahead and follow the track through rough pasture. Turn right as directed later, walking up through a small gate next to a big gate. The track runs towards the farm of **Stool End**, which sits on a slight elevation separating Mickleden and Oxendale. Turning left through the farmyard brings the walk to a swift end.

**5** Turn right, away from the farm, to follow a stony track uphill. Keep left at a junction, avoiding the path to the right, which climbs The Band to reach Bowfell. Walk gently down the track and go through a kissing gate beside a big gate in **Oxendale**. Follow the track until it reaches a drystone-walled sheepfold and go through it using two small gates. Walk as far as a footbridge spanning **Oxendale Beck** and enjoy views of the high fells.

> *ⓘ Beatrix Potter is credited with saving the indigenous Herdwick sheep, which were in danger of being displaced by more profitable breeds.*

*Herdwick sheep are a distinctive Lake District breed*

*Stool End – a Herdwick farm*

**6** Retrace your steps through the sheepfold and back to the farm of **Stool End**. Go through a gate and walk through the farmyard as directed. Leave the farm by walking along its tarmac access road, passing through fields to reach a gate and a minor road. Walk straight ahead along the road to finish near the **Old Dungeon Ghyll Hotel**.

### – To shorten

Leave out the paths leading to the heads of Mickleden and Oxendale by turning left at the drystone wall part-way through Waypoint 2, and left again at Stool End at Waypoint 5. This gives a short circular route of less than 4km.

### Langdale stone axes

High on Pike o' Stickle and Harrison Stickle is a band of hard, fine-grained volcanic rock that was deemed, in Neolithic times, to be ideal for the production of stone axes. These were roughly hewn on site, then taken out of the area for polishing.

*The path crosses boulders in Stickle Ghyll*

# WALK 14
## Stickle Tarn

| | |
|---|---|
| **Start/finish** | New Dungeon Ghyll Hotel, Great Langdale |
| **Locate** | LA22 9JX ///mended.establish.rewrites |
| **Cafes/pubs** | Pub and restaurant at the New Dungeon Ghyll Hotel and Lanty Slee's |
| **Transport** | Daily buses from Ambleside to New Dungeon Ghyll |
| **Parking** | Pay and display near New Dungeon Ghyll Hotel |
| **Toilets** | Close to Lanty Slee's |

**Time** 2¼hr
**Distance** 4.5km (2¾ miles)
**Climb** 400m

**A steep and rugged climb past waterfalls leading to a walk around a scenic tarn**

Stickle Tarn is a popular, scenic tarn high on the Langdale Pikes. The climb up to it is steep and rocky in parts, with a bit of hands-on scrambling required, so take breaks at intervals to admire lovely waterfalls in Stickle Ghyll. (After heavy rain it might not be possible to cross the upper part of Stickle Ghyll.) The tarn is a lovely spot to enjoy a picnic, and you can walk all the way round its shoreline.

*An obvious path climbs uphill on steep slopes of bracken*

87

*Looking across Stickle Tarn to Harrison Stickle and Pavey Ark*

## WALK 14 – STICKLE TARN

**1** Start at the bus stop or car park near the **New Dungeon Ghyll Hotel**. Pass between the hotel and Stickle Cottage, through a gate signposted as a public bridleway. Continue up through a gateway gap in a drystone wall then walk upstream along a path that becomes stone-paved. Simply follow the path alongside **Stickle Ghyll** to reach a footbridge.

**2** Cross the footbridge, stay on the path and further uphill cross a stile over a fence. Keep climbing steadily, taking breaks to admire the many cascades in the stream. The path eventually reaches a rocky area, where you should pause and work out the best route. If other walkers are there, watch how they use their hands as well as their feet, and pick what seems to be the easiest way. Remember that you need to come back this way later, scrambling down the rock. The path leads towards the stream and is quite rugged in places.

**3** Cross the stream by stepping on big boulders, bearing in mind that this might be impassable after heavy rain. Once across, the path climbs another steep and rugged slope, leading to a stone dam that holds **Stickle Tarn** in place.

Looking across the water, the rock face of Pavey Ark rises dramatically, and people might be spotted

*Looking down Stickle Ghyll along Great Langdale*

*The first of many waterfalls passed along the course of Stickle Ghyll*

> ⓘ *The 'Langdale Pikes' is the collective name for two or more of the following summits – Harrison Stickle, Pike o' Stickle, Pavey Ark and Loft Crag.*

crosses a boulder-strewn slope at the foot of **Pavey Ark**. Later, it is easier to follow the path as it crosses the foot of Harrison Stickle, returning to the dam.

**scrambling slowly across it, following a diagonal line known as Jack's Rake.**

**4** To walk round the tarn, cross the outflowing stream first, but only if this can be done without getting wet feet. After a dry spell there are usually plenty of stones underfoot. Follow a path hugging the shoreline, later crossing an inflowing stream. The path narrows and becomes vague as it

**5** All that remains is to retrace your steps faithfully back downhill, taking particular care on that part where you need to pick a way down the short rocky slope. Follow the path all the way back to the **New Dungeon Ghyll Hotel**.

### − To shorten
Omit the walk around Stickle Tarn, saving well over 1km (30min).

### + To lengthen
Follow the path from the New to the Old Dungeon Ghyll Hotel for just under 1.5km (45min).

## Stickle Tarn

Stickle Tarn was once smaller, but a stone-built dam enlarged it in 1838. This was constructed to maintain a regular flow of water along Great Langdale Beck, which was in turn used at gunpowder works between Chapel Stile and Elterwater.

# WALK 15
## Blea Tarn

| | |
|---|---|
| **Start/finish** | Bus shelter near Old Dungeon Ghyll Hotel, Great Langdale |
| **Locate** | LA22 9JY ///points.catch.polka |
| **Cafes/pubs** | Pub and restaurant at Old Dungeon Ghyll Hotel |
| **Transport** | Daily buses from Ambleside to Old Dungeon Ghyll |
| **Parking** | Pay and display at Old Dungeon Ghyll Hotel and Blea Tarn |
| **Toilets** | Old Dungeon Ghyll Hotel |

**Time** 2hr
**Distance** 5km (3 miles)
**Climb** 175m

**A climb featuring splendid views of the fells and a walk round a scenic tarn**

This walk starts near the historic Old Dungeon Ghyll Hotel, famed among fellwalkers and rock climbers. There are splendid views of the Langdale Pikes on the initial climb and final descent. The circuit around Blea Tarn includes fine views of the tarn and surrounding fells. A much shorter walk around the tarn is possible by starting from its car park.

*Looking back to Mickleden, flanked by Bowfell and the Langdale Pikes*

*A clear path descends towards Blea Tarn*

**1** Start at the bus shelter near the **Old Dungeon Ghyll Hotel** and follow the road further, soon turning left. Cross a river and turn left to enter the Great Langdale Campsite. Watch for a marker post and little footbridge on the right. Follow a path through a wood, climbing to pass through two kissing gates. Go up a grassy slope, then through another kissing gate into a small forest.

**2** Leave the forest through a kissing gate and climb an obvious winding path up an open fellside. Remember to turn round to admire the Langdale Pikes and other fells. This path, reconstructed after decades of heavy use, leads to a kissing gate at the top of the Blea Tarn pass at 224m. Cross the road to continue, bearing in mind that the route returns to this point later.

**3** A signpost points the way through a gate towards the distant Wrynose Pass. An obvious gravel path runs downhill, uphill and downhill again. Go through a gate into a forest and pass close to the waters of **Blea Tarn**. The path soon reaches a footbridge at the outflow from the tarn.

**4** Turn left to cross the footbridge and follow a path uphill to go through a gate. Splendid views stretch across the tarn to the Langdale Pikes. Feel free to picnic on the grass or paddle in the water. A further gate leads onto a road with a **car park** immediately opposite.

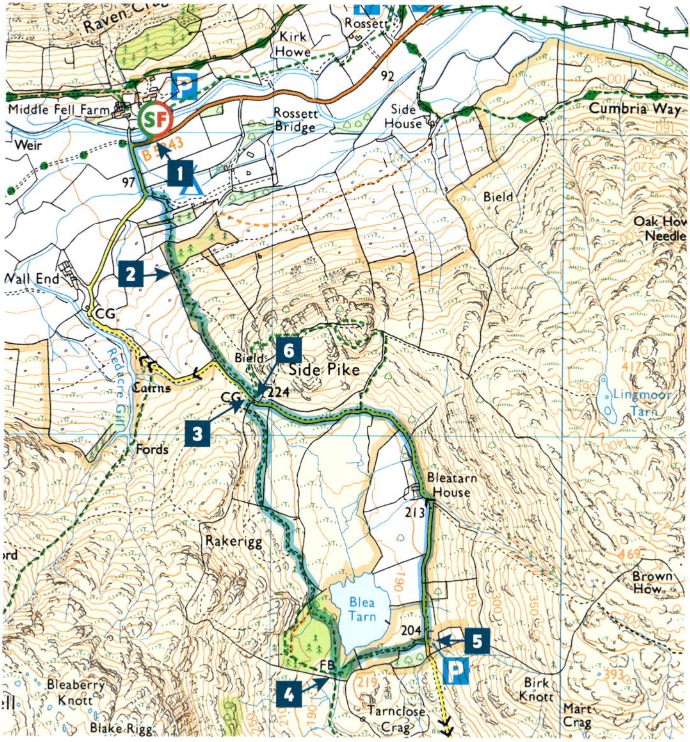

# WALK 15 – BLEA TARN

*View from the road approaching solitary Blea Tarn House*

**SHORT WALKS LAKE DISTRICT – CONISTON & LANGDALE**

**5** Turn left to walk along the road, keeping to the right to face oncoming traffic. The steep and rugged slopes of Lingmoor Fell rise to the right. Solitary Blea Tarn House lies to the left of the undulating road, then **Side Pike** rises to the right. Pass a cattle grid on the top of Blea Tarn pass, at 224m, and immediately turn right through a kissing gate, signposted 'Campsite'.

**6** To finish the walk, simply retrace your steps down to the Great Langdale Campsite and return to the **Old Dungeon Ghyll Hotel**.

> **– To shorten**
>
> Miss out the initial climb from Old Dungeon Ghyll Hotel by starting and finishing at the Blea Tarn car park, almost halving the distance walked.

### Old Dungeon Ghyll Hotel

Commonly referred to as the ODG, the hotel was developed from a farmhouse in the late 19th century. It was frequented by early rock climbers, with some of them cutting their teeth on nearby crags before tackling mountain ranges around the world. Meals and accommodation are available and music sessions sometimes take place in the bar (www.odg.co.uk). The hotel is within easy walking distance of the Great Langdale Campsite.

*The Old Dungeon Ghyll Hotel*

# USEFUL INFORMATION

## Tourism bodies

Cumbria Tourism
www.golakes.co.uk

Lake District National Park
www.lakedistrict.gov.uk

The National Trust
www.nationaltrust.org.uk

## Tourist information centres

Bowness-on-Windermere
tel 0845 901 0845

Keswick tel 0845 901 0845

Ullswater tel 017684 82414

Ambleside tel 015394 32582

Coniston tel 015394 41533

## Weather

Lake District Weatherline
tel 0844 846 2444
www.lakedistrictweatherline.co.uk

## Travel

Traveline
tel 0871 200 2233
www.traveline.info

Stagecoach
www.stagecoachbus.com

Blueworks
www.blueworksph.com

Coniston Launch
www.conistonlaunch.co.uk

Steam Yacht Gondola
www.nationaltrust.org.uk/visit/lake-district/steam-yacht-gondola

## Car parks in Coniston

Coniston tourist information centre
LA21 8EH

Coniston Sports and Social Centre
LA21 8AL

Coniston Old Station
LA21 8HH

Coniston Boating Centre
LA21 8EW

Limited free parking beside the Coppermines road, just after the Ruskin Museum, LA21 8DU

## Buses

The most useful buses for walks in this guidebook are:

Stagecoach 505, daily, from Ambleside, Windermere or Kendal to Coniston and Hawkshead

Blueworks X112 weekdays, from Ulverston to Coniston via Sunny Bank and Torver

Stagecoach 516, daily, from Ambleside, Windermere or Kendal to Skelwith Bridge, Elterwater and Great Langdale

© Paddy Dillon 2024
First edition 2024
ISBN: 978 1 78631 197 9

Printed in China on responsibly sourced paper on behalf of Latitude Press Ltd
A catalogue record for this book is available from the British Library.

© Crown copyright and database rights 2024 OS AC0000810376
All photographs are by the author unless otherwise stated.

# CICERONE

Cicerone Press, Juniper House, Murley Moss, Oxenholme Road,
Kendal, Cumbria, LA9 7RL

www.cicerone.co.uk

### Updates to this Guide

While every effort is made to ensure the accuracy of guidebooks as they go to print, changes can occur during the lifetime of an edition. Any updates that we know of for this guide will be on the Cicerone website (www.cicerone.co.uk/1197/updates), so please check before planning your trip. We also advise that you check information about transport, accommodation and shops locally. We are always grateful for updates, sent by email to updates@cicerone.co.uk or by post to Cicerone, Juniper House, Murley Moss, Oxenholme Road, Kendal, LA9 7RL.

Register your book: To sign up to receive free updates, special offers and GPX files where available, register your book at www.cicerone.co.uk.